How to

By Lora Lake

© 2013. All Rights Reserved.

Cover Image © mageegami - Fotolia.com

Table of Contents

INTRODUCTION 4

CHAPTER 1: BE MINDFUL IN YOUR RELATIONSHIPS 7

- Nice Guys 7
- The Friend Zone 9
- Creating Safe Space 11

CHAPTER 2: KEEP COMMUNICATION LINES CLEAR 12

CHAPTER 3: DON'T SETTLE FOR LESS THAN YOUR WORTH 16

- *Sarcasm* 17
- *Self-Righteousness* 18
- *Entitlement* 19
- *Pressure* 20
- *Resentment* 21
- *Blame* 22
- *Jealousy* 23
- *Pettiness* 24
- *Isolation* 25
- *Deceit* 27
- Stalkers 28
- Mars and Venus 30

CHAPTER 4: KNOW, STATE, AND ENFORCE YOUR BOUNDARIES 31

- To Know 31
- To Dare 33
- To Will..34

CHAPTER 5: TEACH OTHERS HOW TO TREAT YOU 35

CHAPTER 6: OWN YOUR POWER AND YOUR CONSEQUENCE 38

CHAPTER 7: PLAY SAFE AND STAY CONNECTED 42
    RESOURCES 43
CONCLUSION...44

Introduction

There is no question that the world of dating is a different game for women than it is for men. Has it always been this way? Those in the "seduction community" would have you believe so, but are men and women really so different?

Science tells us that deep down, we all want similar things. Our dating styles aren't so disparate because we are so different to seduce, but we have convinced ourselves that men and women are distinct and mysterious creatures. We tell ourselves that all men want sex, all the time, with anyone… and that women need to be at best convinced or at worst coerced into sex of any kind.

Pick up artistry reigns supreme in the world of dating advice for men, despite the fact that it promotes tactics which make assumptions about women's motivations based on out-dated beliefs and can put actual women in physical danger of being "targeted" and exploited.

With this comprehensive and concise eBook you will learn how to find the nice guy in the crowd of "Nice Guys". You will find the strength to empower yourself, to call someone out on inappropriate dating behaviour instead of being manipulated by it, and to recognize tactics designed to circumvent your consent. The only way to avoid being hurt by a jerk is to avoid jerks.

Don't you wish it was that easy?

Barring some serious advances in technology or a breakout of psychicism, you can't just peer inside another person's mind to understand their thoughts and motivations. But a little bit of awareness can go a long way, not only to helping your love life, but to spread the word to socially awkward people everywhere that creepy is not the new sexy.

You can learn the art of seduction without giving up your moral compass and you can expect your lover to be as concerned with your consent as they are with their desire. Neither of these things are unreasonable or impossible tasks!

The rules of the road are simple:

- Be Mindful in Your Relationships
- Keep Communication Lines Clear
- Don't Settle for Less
- Know, State and Enforce Your Boundaries
- Teach Others How to Treat You
- Own Your Power and Consequence
- Play Safe and Stay Connected

You can't control the entire world, but what is within your control can improve your attitude and your approach when it comes to making love connections, drastically improving your odds of meeting someone right for you, instead of someone for right now. Whether you are looking for an occasional lover or a long-term commitment, you don't have to settle for someone who isn't interested in a full, conscious, enthusiastic experience! Sex for pleasure, sex for comfort, sex for love, no matter what your reasons, you deserve the utmost respect and nothing less.

Isn't it time you got what you deserve?

Chapter 1: Be Mindful in Your Relationships

While fodder for hilarious internet memes and fuel for plenty of awkward male anger, the concepts of The Friend Zone and The Nice Guy have been at odds in dating communities for years. Neither is particularly constructive for intimate communication or loving relationships. To put it simply, if you have a "friend" who talks about The Friend Zone or exhibits signs of being a Nice Guy, be aware and prepared to face the issue head on.

Nice Guys

Nice Guys are different from nice guys in one very distinct way. Nice Guys aren't actually nice.

You can spot a Nice Guy by his entitlement. A Nice Guy isn't "nice" to women because they are human beings and deserve the same basic kindnesses as anyone else. A Nice Guy is "nice" because he believes it is the golden ticket to get him into bed, and as such develops a bigger sense of entitlement to sex with every act of "kindness" he performs.

Perform is the key word here. Nice Guys are putting on an act. They may not realize it, but they bear a transactional view of sex that gives them the impression that there is some magic combination of actions they can perform, some random set of buttons they can push that will ultimately pop open the puzzle box that is you, giving them access to the coveted sex treasure inside.

Instead of viewing their potential partners as collaborative participants, a mythology of women as the magical gatekeepers pervades. Your body is seen as an obstacle to the succulent treat inside.

Nice Guys play games as if you are The House and all other men are other players vying for the same payout. Actual nice guys, if they play games at all, play the kind where you get to decide on the rules and the prizes together.

The Friend Zone

In seduction community lingo and now the internet at large, The Friend Zone is a mythical land in relationships where men go when they have embraced the idea that being Nice Guys should earn them sexual points. Whether he views his friendly efforts as a pathway to spontaneous sexual combustion, or instead simply harbours growing resentment about his unvoiced feelings not being addressed, the situation threatens to boil over if one of you doesn't take the lead.

Nice Guys are "nice" to women so they can get sex. If women are nice back, but don't share their desire for sex, she has put him in the Friend Zone and becomes an object of blame instead of lust. The horrid "friend zone" is the terrible second prize a Nice Guy gets when he fails at attaining the super awesome first prize of sex. And Nice Guys hate coming in second.

Is He In "The Friend Zone" Alone?

Recent studies have shown that men in friendships are not only more likely to be attracted to their female friends than women are to male friends, but they also have a tendency to overestimate the level of attraction those female friends feel toward them.

If you get the vibe that one of your male friends is attracted to you, don't just ignore it and hope it goes away. If you aren't interested and don't feel the same attraction, tell him. He needs to hear that you recognize his feelings, but don't share them. He also needs to know that if friendship with you is contingent on you sharing his feelings, you can't be friends. Period.

Friends who demand that you feel a certain way about them don't make great comrades, or wonderful partners for that matter. When you are attracted to someone, you want to be with someone who loves and cares for you because you're you and not as collateral for a sexual transaction.

If he isn't obvious about his attraction, watch out for:

- guy friends who feel "taken advantage of" after offering you emotional or physical support
- men who tend to obsess over other women, particularly close friends, as a trend
- dates who say anything like, "Well, I bought you dinner, so…"
- jealous behaviour of any kind, especially violent or aggressive outbursts, but even "jokes"
- unprovoked concern about your love life or your sex life, despite your own discomfort
- regular complaining that women just don't realize or appreciate what a "great guy" he is
- habitually crossing physical boundaries or invading personal space despite protests
- attempting to explain away "creepy" behaviour as harmless, instead of apologizing

There is only one effective way to deal with a Nice Guy and that is to be completely and utterly clear. Say no. Say it loud and clear. Say it so he really hears it. Then make sure he knows that he isn't going to change your mind, and moreover, that if being friends with you is contingent on you changing your mind, he should get out of your life now, today, for good.

Creating Safe Space

One of the most difficult situations that arises from the appearance of a Nice Guy is that usually, he has other people convinced of his "niceness" as well. If this "friend" of yours is a regular member of your social circle, removing yourself from his presence can be a problem.

If you aren't keen to completely end all communication or give your shared friends ultimatums, at the very least have a sit down with some of the people you both have relationships with and ask them to have some words with him. If you can't convince him that his behaviour is a problem and that your interests lie elsewhere, perhaps some of the men in his life can talk some sense into him.

Friends don't let friends be creepy. Pass it on.

Chapter 2: Keep Communication Lines Clear

Often media focuses on the experience of waiting for the phone call after a date, obsessing over the phone hoping for even a short text or a few words of encouragement. But what happens when someone you've met cares too much about "keeping in touch" with you?

You can use a throw-away email account for your online dating and even get a special untraceable cell phone for your first point of contact if you are having a particularly difficult time with bad dates and overzealous texters. But for most of us, the phone is our main point of contact when it comes to organizing and planning those very first "getting to know you" dates. You probably can't avoid occasionally giving your phone number to someone you later wish didn't have it.

While frequent text messages or phone calls from a date might simply belie a bit of nervousness on their part, some men may take this constant contact too far. Someone who demands that you respond to them on their schedule, who needs to know where you are and what you are doing at all times, or who continues to send you messages that make you uncomfortable after you have expressed your feelings, does not respect your boundaries.

So how do you go about expressing your feelings in such a touchy situation?

Let's look at a few different situations and how you can deal when someone else obviously can't.

1. He Just Won't Shut Up

Unless this is paired with one or both of the next two situations, you can file this under "annoying" and go about communicating your annoyance in whatever way suits you best. Depending on your relationship with this guy, it could play out in a number of different ways. You can flat out tell him to stop calling and texting you so much, or be subtle about the fact that he's just a little too eager for your taste. You can let it leak to a mutual friend that his communication habits are bordering on (or crossing directly into the realm of) creepiness. You can block his number, his email and his Facebook account, and never speak to him again.

I'm sure there are numerous innovative, hilarious or downright cruel things you could do to get the message across, so use your own judgement here. Ultimately, though, get your point across. The longer it goes on, the more he may feel validated in the behaviour, and the higher your cell phone bill is going to be.

2. He is Rude, Gross, Pushy or Sexually Aggressive

Men who send photos of their genitals unsolicited, who expect or demand you to sext with them, who tell "jokes" just to make you uncomfortable and use "negs" or other pick-up techniques to attempt to manipulate your self-worth don't deserve a second of your time, in our opinion, but you might like the occasional dick pic. Either way, if a man doesn't respect your sexual boundaries after being told that he is making you uncomfortable, that isn't likely to improve once the cell phones are gone and you are face to face. Your sexuality is not something you owe to anyone.

3. He "Needs to Know" All About You

Perhaps because you have become the object of his affection, and objects exist to be objectified, he has convinced himself not only that he "needs" but is entitled to every scrap of information about you that he can get his hands on. Like the man who believes he is owed some kind of sexual satisfaction from you, he believes that merely by expressing or bearing an interest in you, he has earned the "prize" of your privacy. He might stalk your online presence, or he may just be unusually interested in where you are and what you're doing at any given time. Don't ever give out more information than you are comfortable with, especially to the wide open audience of the internet.

4. He Really is Just Socially Awkward and Head Over Heels

Honestly, if you like the guy too and the only problem you have with him is how many texts he sends you, tell him so, along with all the things you really do like about him and how much you would like to go out on another date some time...so long as he lets you take the lead. If he can handle that, proceed as desired!

If, on the other hand, you just aren't that into him, but you are convinced he is a really nice guy (and not a Nice Guy as previously discussed), be as gently honest as you can. Explain to him that you aren't interested, but that in the future someone else might be. Give him a few tips on being a bit less clingy, especially if you want to develop or already have a friendship with this guy. Set your boundaries here and now, so that he understands in no uncertain terms the limits of your relationship. He doesn't have to accept your vision of a relationship, but he does have to accept it and decide on his own terms. This is what the real nice guys do.

Chapter 3: Don't Settle for Less than Your Worth

Unfortunately we live in a culture that tends to glorify violence and aggression, to the point that the relationships depicted as the height of romance in many of our favourite stories also meet many of the markers of abusive relationships. It is impossible to completely protect yourself from the possibility of being abused by a partner, but there are some personality traits and signs to watch out for in social settings and early on in a dating relationship that should set off the warning bells.

These hallmark signs of controlling and abusive behaviour patterns may be difficult to see when you have fallen in love with someone, so keep your eyes open in the very early "getting to know you" stages and don't be afraid to seek help if you find yourself in the incredibly challenging situation of ending an abusive or even potentially abusive relationship. See the last chapter for resources, whether you need an action plan, a safe place to stay, or just a sympathetic ear.

Sarcasm

Not everyone who has a sarcastic sense of humour is an abuser, of course, but sarcasm can be used to undermine a person's sense of security, give one person the power to make another feel worse, or simply make it more difficult to know when a person is telling the truth. If your partner is sarcastic enough that you can't always tell when they are being genuine or not, this can make even the simplest communications infinitely more difficult.

Sarcasm is often used as a defence mechanism, brought out when a person feels attacked or insecure, often in a way that deflects attention to someone else's perceived flaws. Alone, a little sarcasm can be perfectly harmless, but if you notice your date using sarcasm as a way to demean you or, more likely in this phase of your relationship, someone else, take heed. A person who need to make someone else look bad in order to make themselves feel good won't spare you when the honeymoon is over.

Self-Righteousness

While we all have bouts of "told you so" syndrome now and again, abusers don't just feel the need to tell you that you are wrong (whether you are or not) but explain why being wrong makes you a bad person. The self-righteous don't just think they have it all figured out, but they know without a shadow of a doubt that this resolve makes them better, greater, smarter, more worthy and more deserving human beings.

Watch out for the debater who feels the need to attack his opponent rather than her argument. Be wary of anyone who needs to be right at all costs, especially if their method for making themselves right involves lashing out into unrelated territory. A man who needs to point out or dwell on the problems of all your past relationships, or his own (and why he thinks this reflects poorly on you or his exes) just to make himself out to be Mr. Right may be hiding under his holier-than-thou attitude a burning desire just to prove you wrong for the sake of being right. Wide, sweeping generalizations about people who he believes all think the same (women, Democrats, doctors, teenagers) point to a similar sense of self-righteousness, which leads directly into the next problem area, self-entitlement.

Entitlement

We have talked a bit about entitled men already, so let's look at the basics. How can you tell someone who's "entitled" from someone who just wants a lot from life? Baby boomers think that entire younger generations are "entitled" simply because they believe they can be happy now, instead of miserable until retirement. There is certainly nothing wrong with expecting things from life! An entitled man, one who exhibits an abuser's tendencies, is a guy who thinks that other people owe him something of themselves just because he is so awesome.

Does he think every woman in the room is looking at him? Does he believe that buying you dinner means he has won the right to the sexy treasure? Does he say things like, "Does she even know who I am?" or "What does it take to get a bit of respect around here?" Watch how he speaks to the people around you, especially those in service positions, like wait staff, personal assistants, shop clerks and bank tellers. If he calls his assistant "hun" or tips poorly even if the service was great and he has the money to spend, it may be time to have a sit down with him about privilege and power. A man who thinks feminists have ruined his sex life and can't recognize his own privileges isn't ready to collaborate in a relationship.

Pressure

It should be obvious, but a man who can't take no for an answer isn't a man to make your life with, or a second date for that matter. Whether the pressure comes from outright attempts to connive or convince you, or sneakier tactics that seek to put you in an uncomfortable or difficult situation so that a sleep over is your only option, there is little love waiting with a man who can't respect your boundaries or desires.

What kind of person wants to have sex with someone who doesn't want to have sex with them? Think about that for a moment the next time pressure tactics come into play. In fact, it doesn't even have to be about sex. Sure, it's nice to try to bring a bit of adventure into a relationship, but if your partner is always taking the lead on dates, doesn't let you pick a restaurant, or is constantly trying to goad you into doing things that make you uncomfortable, he is not someone who will help you to grow as a person. While we all should take the opportunity to step outside our comfort zones now and again, it should be on your own terms, not something you are forced into for the sake of love.

Resentment

On the other end of pressure are those who will punish you for taking a big step. A partner who holds onto resentment, whether based on an actual breach of trust or not, does not have the skills and maturity for long-term growth in a relationship. Especially when resentment is unfounded, misplaced blame, an abuser can use these feelings to justify horrendous behaviour. You are not beholden to anyone. An abuser may even resent your accomplishments. Watch for the difference between resentment and genuine concern. Your lover may be truly worried that your new job will take away your time together, so coming up with a plan to ensure that you still get all your requisite cuddle time is in order! If your date, instead, seems to be grasping at reasons to hate you for your new job, look for ways that your accomplishments seem to damage their self-esteem.

Often we speak of abusers as if they have perpetually low self-esteem, but this is only partially true. An abuser's esteem is tightly linked to the self-esteem of his victims, whoever they may be. The worse the people around him feel about themselves, the better he feels. Conversely, the better those in his world seem to be doing in their own lives, the worse he feels about his. An abuser's sole prerogative then becomes making everyone else around him as miserable as possible.

Blame

Since an abuser is so tied up in everyone else just to feel something good about himself, it becomes incredibly easy for him to blame everyone but himself for the bad things that happen in life. Things don't ever just happen to an abuser. Days, weeks, even months can pass while a self-pitying individual builds up in their head the reason that the world is responsible for their despair. Some of the men who have lived socially isolated or awkward lives have developed this sense of blame and directed it towards women in a wide blanket. These men, drawn to women sexually but still blaming them for the suffering if their youth (as if everyone else had it so easy in high school), can lash out in a number of ways.

They may turn to pick up artistry as a way to become something that women crave, but they sometimes also develop an attitude of conquering: they can "show" all those women from before, if they can "show" enough women now that they are sex-worthy. This, of course, generally means tricking as many women as possible into sex with no intent of ever calling back. Some men, however, aren't happy with a single conquest. An abuser not only blames the people in his lives, but seeks to control them. If he is in complete control of every action you make, he can be sure that you don't mess up his life. And when he loses control, as he invariably will, he can return right back to blame.

Jealousy

People say that jealousy is normal. Not everyone experiences jealousy the same way, so it is important to have conversations with your lovers about what they are comfortable with and around. Unrealistic expectations are a first sign of bad things to come - any man who says that seeing you having a conversation with another man will make him jealous has issues of his own that need working out. Knowing what the boundaries are in your relationship is important, so there is nothing wrong with a man stating, "such and such makes me feel uncomfortable". On the other hand, acting as if he has a right to tell you what to do based on his discomfort is another thing altogether.

Aggressive displays of jealousy are an especially big warning sign of instability. Unless you are actually, physically in need of help from him, there is no reason why your date should be trying to get between you and another man. Guys who puff up their chest and try to look tough just to try and mark their territory all around you aren't going to back down and give you more freedom when your relationship deepens. If he needs to know where you are all the time, snoops around in your cell phone and emails, or spies on you instead of asking you a direct question, he isn't ready for an adult relationship.

(Note: the same is true for you. If you want to know what kind of porn your boyfriend watches, ask him. Don't start playing Nancy Drew spy girl. If you need to be with someone who will be honest with you about their porn use, and he won't, then you have a decision to make.)

Pettiness

For some of these things, like jealousy and resentment, it can be hard to separate the normal, big stuff that we all feel from time to time, and the over-the-top anger and blame that marks abusive interactions. Pettiness is one major flag. How important is the thing that causes all this anger and strife for your date? Is he justifiably angry about losing his job and just lashing out at someone because he is emotional? It still isn't healthy, or happy, but as a one-time event is probably not the start of an abusive downward spiral. Is he screaming so loud he's hoarse and red-faced because the dog got some mud on the carpet (as dogs are known to do) or because the cable went out just before the game (as the cable sometimes does) - what actual, long-term effects does the problem have on your partner's life?

If your lover is upset over something life changing, you can roll with the punches and deal with the big stuff. But if your date is constantly on the edge of his seat over something minor or inconsequential, it's unlikely that this madness will fade to mellow where your relationship is concerned.

Isolation

The beginning of any loving relationship can feel like a whirlwind of everything-wrapped-up-in-you, where you and your lover are the only two people in the world who matter and you could spend eternity looking into each other's eyes. It feels awesome for a few days, maybe even weeks, but it won't last. Chemically, it can't last. If you are the friend who is constantly ditching her friends whenever the next new beau comes along, that's a problem all of its own.

Isolation makes not only all your wonderful, in-love, ooey-gooey feelings seem like the most powerful force in the universe, but everything else as well. All your bad days can seem like the worst you have ever experienced. Annoyances become loud frustrations, which become screaming arguments. This cycle isn't healthy for anyone. If your lover is extremely resistant to you being in contact with friends and family, going out alone or in groups with other people, you must re-evaluate your priorities. Don't give up on everyone else you care about because your lover doesn't like being alone, or going outside, or seeing you with other men, or wondering what you're doing with other women. His insecurities aren't your priorities. Don't let anyone cut you off from the people, places and things that make you who you are.

Deceit

Lies can take many forms. Whether your partner lies to protect himself, to get away with something, to simply be cruel or to force your hand somehow, its ultimate consequence is to rob you of your own self-confidence. Every time your partner lies to you, he manipulates you into choosing between trusting him and trusting yourself. Human beings can tell when they are being lied to, and you know what you have seen, said, and experienced. Someone who tries to tell you that they know and understand your experience better than you do doesn't deserve your attention, let alone your love.

Some lies can seem simple and innocuous. You may not need to end things over him lying about his height on his dating profile, but a pattern of even little-white-lies, even if he's telling them to friends or co-workers instead of you, calls into question his integrity and honesty with everyone in his life. Don't give your trust away blindly, especially to someone who gives you reason to be more cautious.

Stalkers

Not all abusers exhibit the same kind of obsessive behaviour as stalkers, and not all stalkers show these same abusive traits. In fact, many women find themselves victims of stalkers without ever even meeting their abuser. In a digital age, keeping tabs on someone from afar has become a field of knowledge all its own. Here are some ways to spot stalking behaviour early.

1. "Cyber-Stalking" - he knows everything you've ever posted to your online profiles, watches your Facebook relentlessly, possibly from a fake account, keeps tabs on your Twitter account and is desperate to see all your FourSquare details so he knows exactly where you are at all times. If you are in the habit of "friending" people who aren't your friends, you may want to clean up your social networks and enable some privacy filters.

2. Lurking - he just happens to be "around" all the time, by your work, your favourite coffee shop, the places you have mentioned that you go online, etc. If you go to the same gym, that might just be a coincidence, but showing up there at the same time three days a week might be a bit more.

3. Phone Calls and Texts - whether phone calls with no answer or just weirdly inappropriate messages and texts, once this guy has your phone number he is unlikely to stop using it. Use your block functions wisely.

4. Gifts - a bouquet of flowers on an actual date is a great surprise, but showing up with a promise ring at your door three weeks later shows at the very least a severe lack of impulse control.

5. Insertions - does he just happen to show up in the right place, at the right time, with just the right thing you need? Car suddenly stop working and he's there with a boost? Rainy day and he arrives with an umbrella? Creating situations in which he can rescue you is an obvious sign of disordered thinking when it comes to love and relationships. Do not engage!

6. Lashing Out - people with this kind of mindset often, ultimately, become angry and lash out when their victims do not respond in the way that they have conjured in their fantasies. Stalking behaviour can lead to more cruel forms of harassment as well as violence. Do not let stalking go on ignored. Tell someone, anyone who can help. See the last chapter for resources.

7. It All Adds Up - any kind of cumulative, unwanted contact or attention qualifies as stalking. Call the police or talk to someone in your local violence prevention communities to help you report the behaviour.

Mars and Venus

I have written this advice specifically for women meeting new men, but men do not have a monopoly on abusive relationships. Do any of these aspects of personality resonate with you? Do you ever find yourself blaming people for your own mistakes, or for things that just...happen? Do you get upset over petty things, or pressure people into things they don't especially enjoy doing? Do you overuse sarcasm, hold on to grudges, or try to make people feel badly for holding a different opinion than you? Do you lie? Have you spent hours perusing old photos on some guy's Facebook profile or called someone and hung up?

No one can write you a full-proof guarantee for never meeting or falling in love with an abusive person. But you can do your best to avoid being an abuser yourself, and learn how to spot someone who, at the very least, isn't ready for a calm, communicative and collaborative relationship like you.

Chapter 4: Know, State, and Enforce Your Boundaries

There are three aspects to proper boundary maintenance when it comes to relationships:

- knowing what your boundaries are
- daring to speak them out loud
- engaging only with people who respect them

As a woman, you may have been taught that your boundaries don't really matter, or that speaking about your sexual needs and desires is somehow unsexy or "slutty" - banish these thoughts. Any guy who thinks it's "unladylike" for you to talk about what you want in a sexual relationship can keep it between himself and his palms. If you're going to get what you want, you need to want it like you mean it!

To Know

Knowing what your own boundaries are sounds like it should be easy, but most of us approach life with the idea that we'll know our boundaries when we bump up against them. Unfortunately it is usually someone else who does the bumping and we are left with the emotional bruises to show for it.

Spend some time - not just minutes, but hours over many days, on an ongoing basis - working through all the ideas and assumptions you have about relationships and sex. Think about what you want out of your relationships, what you need and what you can give, what you are willing to do and what you have no interest in right now. Think about both "hard" boundaries, things on which you are not willing to compromise, and "soft" boundaries, or the things that you might find changing with the right person. Your boundaries might be sexual, or have to do with privacy, personal space, time, spirituality, family, or other commitments. Think about the things in your life that you consider priorities and how they fit into your current and future relationships.

Sit down and take a Kink Checklist before you start exploring sex with new partners. Knowing what you like is the first step to getting it! You might be interested in trying out a few things that you hadn't even thought about before, or you may just need the confidence and vocabulary that comes along with taking a comprehensive quiz to be able to communicate your sexual desires to partners, new and familiar.

To Dare

Of course, knowing what you want does not automatically beam it directly into the brain of your lovers. If only we had the technology! No, the process of communicating desire is one which we often fear is fraught with peril. We have been told for so long that sex talk is weird, or awkward, or cheesy, or pornofied. Well fear not, because contrary to popular opinion, talking about sex is actually sexy! Can you believe it?

The basis of consent culture, which values collaborative sex between enthusiastic lovers, is in the ability to communicate desire. You need to be able to say what you want to do, or have done to you, in actual words. Out loud. So that someone else can hear you. If the idea terrifies you, take some time to practice beforehand. Look yourself in the mirror and talk about the desires you discovered through completing your Kink Checklist, or describe a specific fantasy that you have. When we first begin to practice, couples often think about seeking consent as asking permission. Instead, focus inward not on asking if you can do something specific to your partner, but expressing your desire.

When you say, "I want to feel _____" or "I would love to kiss your _____" then your lover has the opportunity to either respond by fulfilling your desire, or presenting a desire of their own. You may not always have the same desires, but by stating the things you each desire most, you can certainly find a way for both of you to find pleasure!

To Will

Making the pleasure part actually happen may be easier said than done. Not all of our fantasies are realistic, especially if we are new to kinky play or trying out fantasies that we have only ever dreamt of before. Instead of jumping right into acting on your desires, why not try a little mutual masturbation first?

This sex act is incredibly low-risk, high-heat, super duper sexy and way creative. You can talk about your fantasies and your desires, your limits and your boundaries, all the sexy things you want to do or have done, all from the comfort of bed. Lie back and watch your lover do the same, talk about the possibilities and the boundaries while you get worked into a frenzy together! Could it be any hotter?

As a rule, a guy who isn't willing to "settle" for mutual masturbation when you tell him how hot it would get you to watch him while you talk about your fantasies doesn't sound like he's in it for the long haul. If it's "intercourse or bust" then tell him where he can go bust.

Chapter 5: Teach Others How to Treat You

This one is simple. When a person treats you a certain way and you accept, perpetuate, or otherwise enable that treatment, it is easier for them to treat you that way the next time. This isn't about blame, but understanding the minds of users and abusers. It is much easier for someone who cares only about themselves to justify hurting you for their gain when you remain in a relationship with someone who hurts you. Abuse is a sick cycle that does not remedy itself.

This isn't about the old adage to "treat others as you would like to be treated." Instead you should be treating others as they desire to be treated and requiring that they do the same for you. Read up on things like Gary Chapman's "Love Languages" so you know what kind of behaviour communicates love to you, and so you can practice communicating love in a variety of ways to the new people you meet and find filling important roles in your life.

You are responsible for communicating to someone when their behaviour is hurtful to you. If a guy is being creepy, tell him so. Use subtle means if you feel inclined, but don't let it continue unchallenged. If your partner is being disrespectful, chances are they aren't even aware they are doing it. Tell them so. Don't assume that your lover knows what makes you feel good and what makes you feel bad. You do not have to accept any kind of poor treatment, but do not stay and expect change if you aren't willing to make the need for change known.

Studies have looked at different aspects of the ways that partners can encourage change in each other. In general, people who believe that it is possible for us human beings to change ourselves have better long-term relationships. These people, however, also have difficult recognizing that change can be very difficult. Believing that your partner can grow and change as a person doesn't make it any more likely to happen. If the person you are seeing isn't the person you want them to be, and has no desire to be the person you want them to be, nothing you believe about them is going to change that fact. Remember that change is difficult, but you are only responsible for yourself. Be vocal about your needs and don't accept less.

Do you consider yourself a kind person? What does kindness mean to you?

Being kind, in relationships and love, should be about being the best person you can be and loving someone enough to allow them to be the best person that they can be. But remember, you can't force someone to be your vision of their best. What does this mean for you? That the truest kindness you can do in a failing relationship is to let someone go.

When you consider yourself to be a kind and loving person, you may find that others read you as someone they can take advantage of, whether consciously in the case of the predatory type, or subconsciously as they seek out support for their own failing egos. Don't let yourself be used. Once you know what your boundaries are, don't compromise them for fear of not being "nice" enough. You do not have to be sugar and spice.

Guys who are constantly forgetting their wallet aren't worth your time - if he really can't afford the place you're going, he should have the decency to say so and plan something on the cheap instead. If he only ever calls you at the last minute for a booty call, well, it's up to you if you're into it, but don't expect more than he's willing to offer! Don't do things you don't want to do, in the hopes that it will be enough to win him over into being someone better. Tell him what you want. If he isn't willing to give you what you want, you don't owe him anything. Find someone who shares your needs and desires!

Chapter 6: Own Your Power and Your Consequence

When most people hear the word "assertive" they think about "aggressive" - in your face, big and loud, over the top and ready to take on the world. Well, the last part might apply to both, but it certainly isn't the rule.

Being assertive is all about knowing and getting what you want. We discussed this in relation to boundaries, sexual kinks, relationship desires and needs, but what about in the dating game, out in the field? What does it look like to be an assertive woman out at the club or down at the bar, or even in line at the grocery store?

In the pick-up artist's seduction game, women tend to be portrayed as passive objects. There are a variety of techniques he is taught that he can use on you, one of which is bound to work, he is assured, while you are expected to sit idly by and wait to be acted upon. Well the future of dating is not for the passive. If you want to find men who aren't the overly-aggressive assholes from the seduction school, you need to learn to make a first move.

This isn't about trying to pick people up. You are an amazing woman who can talk to people who look interesting, because you have the confidence and cool to start a conversation! Right?

Okay, maybe you are and maybe you aren't. The real question is, do you want to be?

Here are some things to think about before you go out next:

1. What makes you awesome?

Seriously. Come up with the ten or twenty coolest things about you (even if they are only in your head - really) and write them all down in a long list. How many ways can you think of to show off each of these awesome things? Try to come up with at least one or two conversation starters for each of your "Awesomes".

2. Do awesome things.

Can't think of anything? Start journaling and each morning, try to come up with a short story about yourself doing something awesome. Think about all the awesome things you would really like to do, then go and do them! While you're out and about doing your awesome things, see if you can start up a conversation with a stranger!

3. Talk to people.

Don't start with the seriously hunky guy at the bookstore that you've been drooling over for the past year, unless you really crave a challenge. Instead just start striking up genuine conversations with random people you meet anywhere - at the grocery store, at the library, on the street, at the office. Talk to the person who delivers your mail, chat with customer service people on the phone while they're looking up your information, smile and be friendly with your wait staff and your bartender. Give your conversation a personal touch and try to go above and beyond "Hello" and "How are you?" and "Fine weather today!"

4. Be yourself... from the future.

Okay, so maybe you don't actually know who you are going to be in the future, but the point is that when it comes to seduction, to dating, to being the awesome and assertive woman you want to be, who can stand up to the jerks out there and flirt with the amazing men you meet - who that woman is, is entirely up to you.

You get to decide. Right now, today, you can remake yourself and become anyone you want to be. Do you want to be the brazen seductress? Go be her! Get out the amazing dress, go to a new place where you can dance the night away and talk to new people. If you're having trouble getting started, think about where you might meet other people like the woman you want to be. Dance class? Yoga? A women's business circle? Personal development courses? Book clubs? Go where the future you already hangs out!

5. Stand up to jerks.

Say something. When someone makes a sexist joke, or exhibits signs of being emotionally or physically abusive, or tries to undermine your confidence and power… don't let it go by unnoticed. Say something. Make your opinions heard. Don't let yourself be pushed around and be prepared to take care of yourself. Have money to get your own cab after a night out, if you aren't driving yourself. Pay attention to your surroundings and know where you are. Party with friends, because friends are awesome! Look out for the people you love and have people in your life who you trust to look out for you.

Chapter 7: Play Safe and Stay Connected

One of the best ways to live a safe and healthy life is to always stay connected. Isolation, whether you are single or in a relationship, begins an immediate recipe for disaster. Friends, family and loved ones can support you in your search for love and your quest for self-improvement. They can tell you when things don't seem quite right from their perspective and see, from a unique angle, things that you might miss when you are falling head-over-heels in love with someone who may not be ready for your love.

Gather together a close community. Spend time outside of the house with people who care about you on a regular basis. Cultivate friendships however you can. If you cannot maintain friendships, perhaps you aren't ready for love yet either. Find things that interest you, check your "awesome things" list and go out to meet some new people. Making friends can be as nerve-wracking as meeting new lovers, but it is worth it!

Resources

When you head out on a date with a stranger or someone you have met only online, be sure to do so in a public place and set up a "safe call" - someone who knows what you are doing and will check in on you if you don't get back to them to let them know all has gone well.

Pick Up Artists at the Geek Feminism Wiki:
http://geekfeminism.wikia.com/wiki/Pick_Up_Artists

Feminist Critics "Seduction Community and Pick Up Artists" page:
http://www.feministcritics.org/blog/about/seduction-communitypickup-artists/

If you are experiencing a domestic violence or stalking emergency, dial 911.

In the US: call the National Domestic Violence Hotline at 1-800-799-7233 (SAFE).
UK: call Women's Aid at 0808 2000 247.
Canada: call the National Domestic Violence Hotline at 1-800-363-9010.
Australia: call 1800RESPECT at 1800 737 732.
Worldwide: visit International Directory of Domestic Violence Agencies for a global list of helplines, shelters, and crisis centers.

Conclusion

You are a strong, confident, beautiful woman and you want to spend your life (or at least a few great nights) with a strong, confident, handsome man who knows exactly how amazing you are. Why leave something like this up to fate? You are a smart lady. You know that you and your lover can and should be equals. You want someone who respects you and desires you at the same time.

So why would you leave your dating future in the hands of guys who think they have the perfect recipe to push your lady-buttons and pop out your lady-sex-prize?

You wouldn't. Because you know better, because you are worth more, because you don't have to. You are not constrained by society telling you that women must be passive, must be chased by men who howl like dogs on your heels. You don't need to wait around for the right guy…in fact, waiting around will only attract the kind of guy who wants a passive partner! You and I both know that isn't who you are - you don't want to be told what to do and what to like, how to date or how to have sex. You want to figure out these things the fun way, don't you?

So focus your energies on finding someone else who has fun like you do. Make a few commitments to change how you date.

1. If you use online dating services, don't spend all your time replying to guys who have made the first move. Be bold! Go out and see if you can find someone more interesting and write that first nerve-wracking letter yourself. Put your bad self out there and see what comes back!

2. Meet new people just because you can. Don't focus on starting up new conversations only with the hottest and most eligible bachelors in the room. Talk to lots of new people, because exposing yourself to new ideas is great for your brain, and because new friends can be just as good, if not better, than a new guy to roll around with in bed.

Most importantly, think for yourself. Love yourself. Love people who love themselves, just the way they are, and for what they can be. Love people who can love you the same way.

Printed in Great Britain
by Amazon